BRIGHT
IDEA
BOOKS

HOW DO
Bionic Limbs
WORK?

by Meg Marquardt

Content Consultant

Gerald E. Loeb, M.D.
Professor of Biomedical Engineering
University of Southern California

CAPSTONE PRESS
a capstone imprint

Bright Idea Books are published by Capstone Press
1710 Roe Crest Drive, North Mankato, Minnesota 56003
www.mycapstone.com

Library of Congress Cataloging-in-Publication Data
Names: Marquardt, Meg, 1986- author.
Title: How do bionic limbs work? / by Meg Marquardt.
Description: North Mankato, Minnesota : Capstone Press, [2019] | Series:
   How'd they do that? | Audience: Grade 4 to 6. | Includes bibliographical
   references and index.
Identifiers: LCCN 2018018708 (print) | LCCN 2018019897 (ebook) | ISBN
   9781543541779 (ebook) | ISBN 9781543541373 (hardcover : alk. paper)
Subjects: LCSH: Prosthesis--Juvenile literature. | Bionics--Juvenile
   literature.
Classification: LCC Q320.5 (ebook) | LCC Q320.5 .M33 2019 (print) | DDC
   617.9--dc23
LC record available at https://lccn.loc.gov/2018018708

Editorial Credits
Editor: Megan Gunderson
Designer: Becky Daum
Production Specialist: Dan Peluso

Photo Credits
Alamy: Mark Thiessen/National Geographic Creative, 26; AP Images: Brian Kersey, 6–7, 8–9, Friso
Gentsch/picture-alliance/dpa, cover; Getty Images: Arnaldur Halldorsson/Bloomberg, 20–21,
Ensar Ozdemir/Anadolu Agency, 24–25, Marwan Naamani/AFP, 11, Ricky Carioti/The Washington
Post, 18–19; iStockphoto: FatCamera, 17, Nanette_Grebe, 30–31, RichVintage, 23, 28; Newscom:
Oleksandr Rupeta/NurPhoto/Sipa U, 5; Science Source: Philippe Psaila, 14–15; Shutterstock
Images: SeventyFour, 12–13

Design Elements: iStockphoto, Red Line Editorial, and Shutterstock Images

TABLE OF CONTENTS

CHAPTER 1

A BRAND-NEW Leg

A man lost his leg in an accident. Later he sits in a doctor's office. He sees a new leg. It was made just for him.

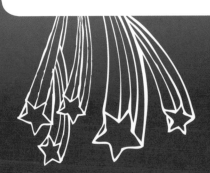

A new leg will help the man walk again.

GAINING A LEG

The leg was built by **engineers**. It is black and silver. It is made of metal and plastic. Inside are wires and computer chips. The leg is **bionic**.

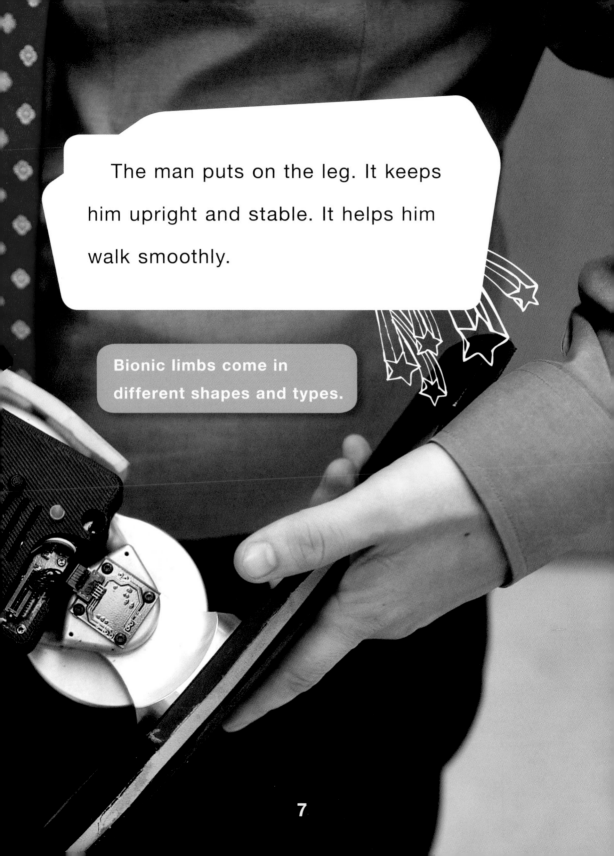

The man puts on the leg. It keeps him upright and stable. It helps him walk smoothly.

Bionic limbs come in different shapes and types.

LEGS OF THE FUTURE

In the future, a bionic leg will be even more special. It will be able to feel the ground. It will send signals directly to the brain.

The man would control the leg with his thoughts. He would feel with his toes again. This is the future of bionic limbs!

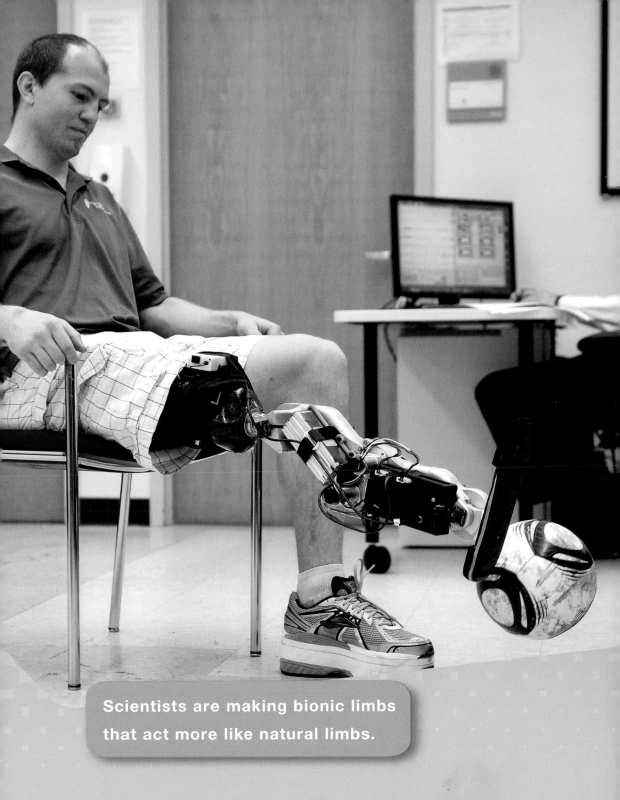

Scientists are making bionic limbs that act more like natural limbs.

CHAPTER 2

WHAT ARE
Bionic
Limbs?

Artificial limbs have a long history. They are also called prosthetic limbs. These were invented in ancient Egypt. A toe is the first known example. It was made of wood and leather.

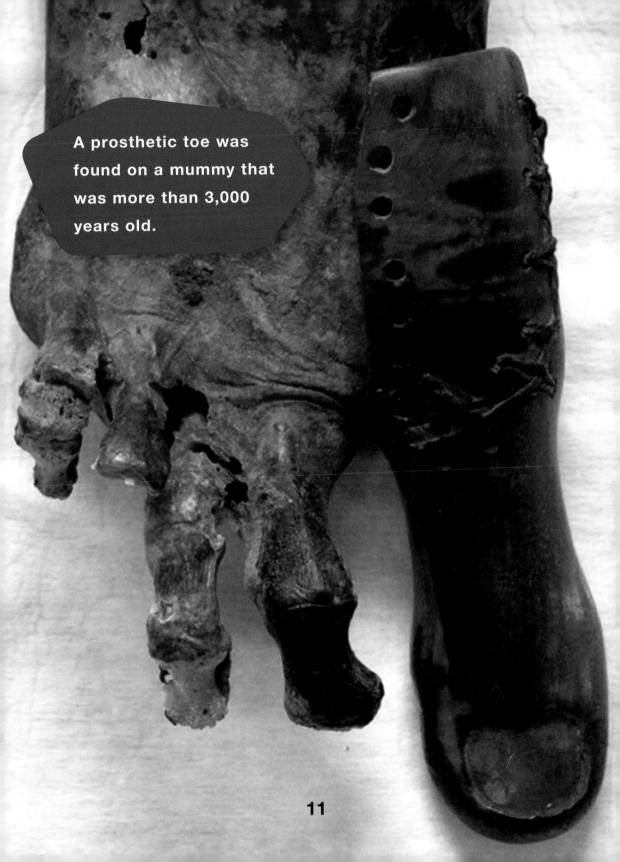

A prosthetic toe was found on a mummy that was more than 3,000 years old.

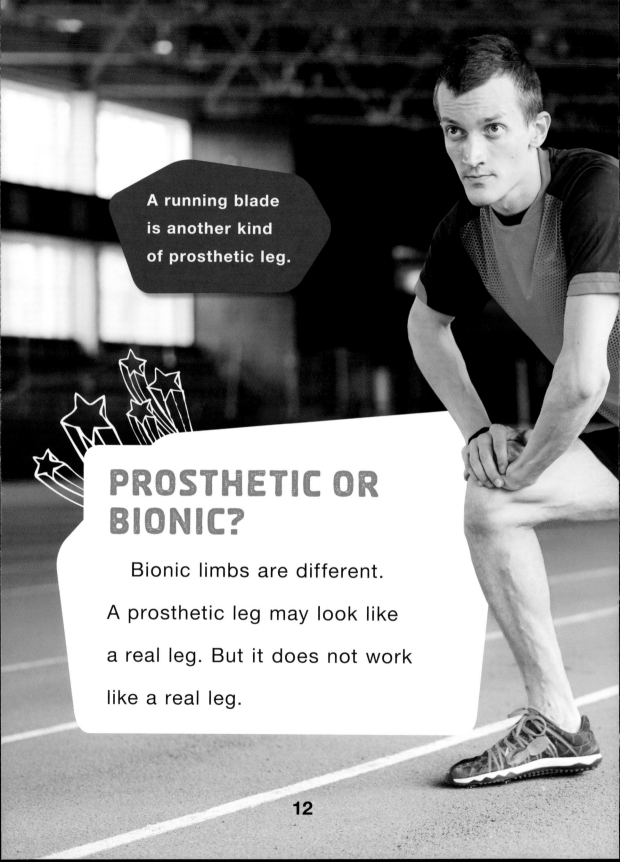

A running blade is another kind of prosthetic leg.

PROSTHETIC OR BIONIC?

Bionic limbs are different. A prosthetic leg may look like a real leg. But it does not work like a real leg.

Bionic legs contain computers, motors, and **sensors**. These things help them work like real legs. They don't just take the place of a leg. They act like one.

A person's arm muscles control her bionic hand.

WHAT'S THAT WORD?

The word *bionic* was first used in the 1960s. It is a mix of two words. *Bio* is for **biology**. *Nic* is for electronics. A bionic limb is the best of both worlds.

WHY NOW?

Bionic limbs are new **inventions**. They didn't exist until the right **technology** was created.

The first one was used in 1993. Since then, engineers have invented many amazing bionic limbs.

CHAPTER 3

BIONIC
Legs

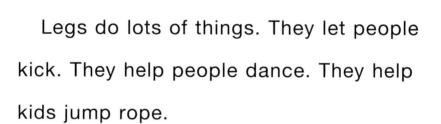

Legs do lots of things. They let people kick. They help people dance. They help kids jump rope.

Legs let kids hang upside down on the playground.

17

WALKING ISN'T EASY

Just plain walking is important too.

Walking might seem easy. But it's not!

Muscles and bones must work together.

To stay balanced you need a brain.

A bionic leg has a tough job.

Bionic legs help a man walk.

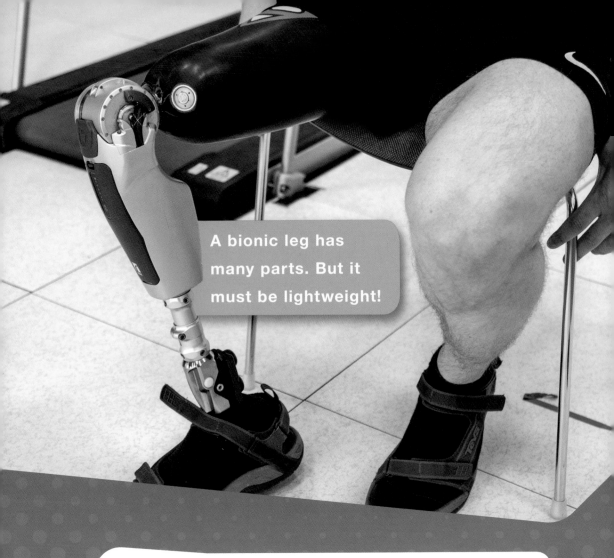

A bionic leg has many parts. But it must be lightweight!

STRONG & LIGHT

A bionic leg needs to be made of special material. It has to last a long time. It can't be too heavy.

BATTERY-POWERED

Today, a bionic leg also needs a battery. The battery powers a motor. The motor acts like a muscle. It pushes the leg forward to walk.

COMPUTERS

Bionic legs also have computers. The computer learns how a person walks. The person uses the leg more. The leg gets better at walking. The computer is a brain for the bionic leg.

CHAPTER 4

BIONIC
Arms

An arm has a lot of jobs. An arm needs to lift, hold, push, and reach things. Arms help people ride bicycles. They swing rackets and bats.

Arms help a kid pitch a baseball.

23

A bionic arm can help a person do delicate tasks like typing.

24

TO FEEL AGAIN

A hand is the most important part of an arm. Fingers give a person a lot of information. A normal prosthetic arm can't do that. But a bionic arm could.

Scientists have created bionic hands that can feel. Each finger has sensors. The fingers sense heat and cold. They also sense soft and hard. Scientists are trying to send that information to the brain.

A person must practice using a bionic limb.

MIND CONTROL

Bionic arms can even be controlled with the mind. The brain sends a message to muscles.

The message goes through to the bionic arm. The arm moves. It's just like a real arm!

LEVELING THE PLAYING FIELD

Bionic limbs help people with **disabilities**. The people can do more activities. Being able to do more helps them get better jobs.

GLOSSARY

artificial
not natural, but made to look like something natural

biology
the science of living things

bionic
relating to body parts that can act normally but are made up of or include electronic parts

disability
a physical or mental condition that limits a person's ability to do various tasks

engineer
a person who designs, builds, and fixes machines

implant
something placed in a person's body by surgery

invention
an original device

sensor
a device that measures heat, motion, moisture, or other conditions

technology
a method or machine created using science

TRIVIA

1. Limbs aren't the only bionic body parts a person can get. There are also bionic eyes.

2. People who are deaf can get a cochlear implant. The cochlea is the part of the ear that hears sound. The implant can let people hear again.

3. Other electronic implants help control parts of the body. A pacemaker makes sure a heart is beating well.

4. Some implants can release medicine. The bionic implant can read if a person needs a dose of medicine. Then it will give a person a dose. This could help someone with a disease like diabetes.

ACTIVITY

You are an engineer who cannot wait to make someone a new limb. However, this person has some special needs. Maybe she is an astronaut. Maybe she is a ballerina. She needs a special limb to do a special job.

Think about a person who does a really cool job. Then imagine she needs a new arm or leg. Do some research into how she does her job. Then come up with a limb that fits her perfectly.

FURTHER RESOURCES

Read about amazing bionic limbs in these sources:

Furstinger, Nancy. *Unstoppable: True Stories of Amazing Bionic Animals*. Boston, Mass.: Houghton Mifflin Harcourt, 2017.

LEGO Makes Everything Better — Even a Prosthetic for Kids
www.wired.com/2015/07/lego-makes-everything-bettereven-prosthetic-kids/

Check out engineering games and events:

Engineering for Kids
http://engineeringforkids.com

Engineering Games
http://pbskids.org/games/engineering

Have a great idea? For this contest, kids create future technology:

ExploraVision
https://www.exploravision.org

INDEX